For Christopher Melling
Thanks Dad

HODDER CHILDREN'S BOOKS

First published in Great Britain in 2002 by Hodder Children's Books
This edition published in 2016 by Hodder and Stoughton

14

Text and illustrations copyright © David Melling, 2002

The moral rights of the author and illustrator have been asserted.

A CIP catalogue record for this book
is available from the British Library.

ISBN 978 0 340 94403 5

Printed in Hong Kong

Hodder Children's Books
An imprint of
Hachette Children's Group
Part of Hodder and Stoughton
Carmelite House
50 Victoria Embankment
London EC4Y 0DZ

An Hachette UK Company
www.hachette.co.uk

www.hachettechildrens.co.uk

Just Like My Dad

David Melling

Hodder
Children's
Books

This is my dad.

One day, I'll have sharp teeth...

...just like my dad.

And spiky hair…

…just like my dad.

I'll grow long nails and a swishy tail...

...just like my dad.

and lick my nose...

...just like my dad.

When I eat my tummy talks...

gurgle

gurgle

…just like my dad's.

And when I lie around being
lazy, my mum says…

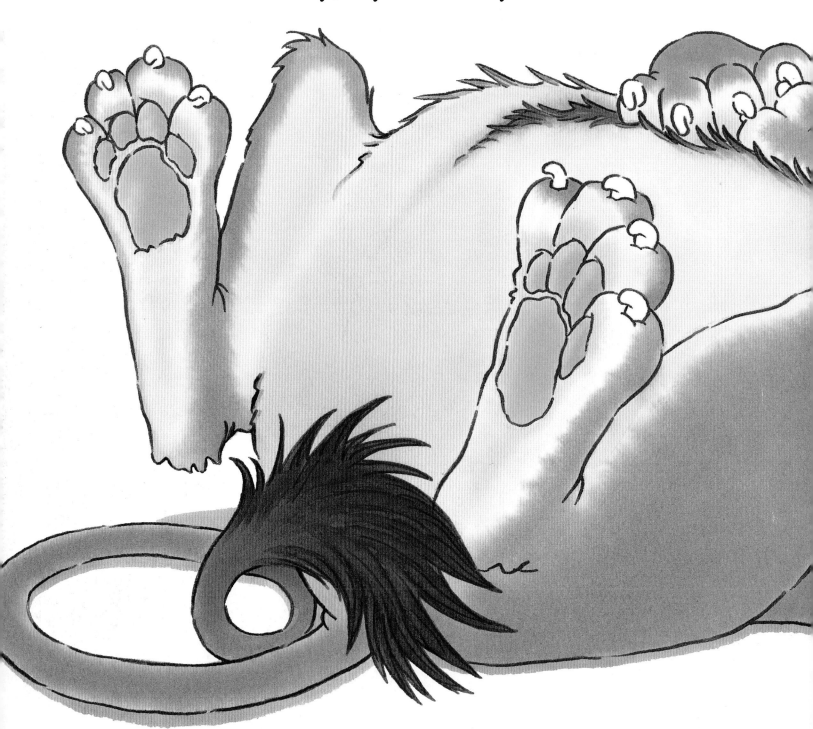

My dad says
I must not be
afraid of
anything...

big...

...or small.

Sometimes my dad can be a little cross…

...but I can make him laugh really loud.

When we play
hide-and-seek with my
friends my dad likes
to go first…

But he's not very good!

Even so, all my friends say,
when they grow up they want to be...

...just like my dad.

Other books by David Melling:

The Kiss That Missed

Good Knight, Sleep Tight

The Three Wishes

Two by Two and a Half

The Scallywags

The Scallywags Blow Their Top

The Tale of Jack Frost

Hugless Douglas

Don't Worry Hugless Douglas

Hugless Douglas and the Big Sleep

We Love You, Hugless Douglas

Happy Birthday, Hugless Douglas

Hugless Douglas Goes to Little School

Just Like My Mum